What the solicitor says about...

Starting Your Business

A practical guide through the legal maze of the early years of business

GWYNETH ALLSOPP

Starting Your Business
A practical guide through the legal maze of the early years of business

©Gwyneth Allsopp

ISBN: 978-1906316-82-2

All rights reserved.

Published in 2011 by HotHive Books, Evesham, UK.
www.thehothive.com

The right of Gwyneth Allsopp to be identified as the author of this work has been asserted by her in accordance with the Copyright, Designs and Patents Act 1988.

A CIP record of this book is available from the British Library.
No part of this publication may be reproduced in any form or
by any means without prior permission from the author.

Printed in the UK by TJ International, Padstow

While every reasonable endeavour has been made to ensure that all information provided in this book is accurate and up to date, Gwyneth Allsopp makes no warranty or representation that this is the case. She makes no guarantee of any specific results from the use of this book. No part of this book is intended to constitute advice and the content of this book should not be relied upon when making any decisions or taking any action of any kind. Always seek legal or other professional advice if you feel you require it.

Contents

About the author 5

Introduction 9

Chapter 1 .... *Make a list* 15

Chapter 2 .... *A crystal clear vision* 27

Chapter 3 .... *Writing a formal business plan* 41

Chapter 4 .... *Cash: borrow safely* 53

Chapter 5 .... *To limit or not to limit* 67

Chapter 6 .... *Leave your present job!* 83

Chapter 7 .... *What is our address?* 97

Chapter 8 .... *Basic contract and a paper trail* 111

Useful contacts 122

Useful reading 123

What people say about Gwyneth 124

About the author

Gwyneth Allsopp

About the author

Thank you for reading this, the first book in the 'What the solicitor says' series. I am sure that if I were you I would want to know who I am, what I have done and my experience.

I have been a solicitor since 1984, over 25 years. In that time I have been employed as a solicitor and I have been in legal partnerships. I have owned and been involved in other businesses and I now own a successful solicitor's practice called The Law Practice (UK) Ltd which began its life just before the recession and has gone from strength to strength. I had a business in the 1990s which grew to employ 20 people in three years.

I am a public speaker at business events and I am a mother of two hopeful teenage boys who keep my feet firmly on the ground.

I have gained extensive experience over the years in court disputes between businesses and in preparing and advising on all the documents and agreements which businesses need. I help with property leases and employment matters.

About the author

I have worked alongside businesses for 25 years. Hundreds of times clients have brought their problems to me. Often I have thought "if only you had talked to me sooner. Things just wouldn't have got this bad!" Often I have sat at my desk listening with my head in my hands in despair. And if I am in despair just listening, the despair of the client can't be imagined.

I hope that you enjoy this book, and the others in the series, and that you gain knowledge and information which helps you run your business without extra stresses.

Gwyneth

Introduction

Your only job is to grow the business

Introduction

This book is a mixture of law, business, common sense and sums. My aim is to give you the sort of good, practical advice that you will find very useful in the early years of your own business, whether as a new business, a franchise or a takeover of an existing business.

This book is a distillation of my personal experiences and those of my clients over the years. I have been a solicitor for over 25 years and in that time I have been privileged to work with many and varied businesses of all types and sizes. Some were in their infancy and others were generations old. Some were very profitable and others, well to put it kindly, not so profitable. I have worked with businesses from all sectors and from all parts of the country. One of my most memorable was a commercial pig farm in Southern Ireland – but that is a different story! I have worked in businesses and I have owned businesses.

And throughout I have been a solicitor. If I am lucky, I get to advise people before they do things and if I am not then I help them pick up the pieces. Personally, I have begun four very different businesses and been the midwife for scores of others.

I considered calling this book *The Unlegal Legal Guide* because I want to give you legal and business information in as clear and concise way as I can with as little legal jargon as possible. Sometimes though, it is unavoidable and so I am going to ask for your understanding now rather than each time I use a legal word or phrase.

I know all too well that there is a special allure to being your own boss, of leaving your job and setting up your own business. And now many people are facing redundancy because of the state of the economy and so are very seriously considering starting their own businesses.

Running your own business is incredibly exciting and rewarding but it is also tiring and stressful. If you thought that you were working long hours as an employee then that will be nothing to the hours which you will work for yourself.

With this book I want to give some practical help and guidance, to provide some answers and some information. Many, many times I have sat at my own desk puzzling over something and thinking to myself *"I wish I knew the answer to that"* or *"I wish I knew someone who could help me with that"*. In my case it is often not a legal issue but a practical business issue, perhaps about sales or buying something we need.

A subtitle for this series of books could be *I Wish I Had Known That*. And as a little start, here are a few sound bites which you may just find useful:

- Expect the unexpected

- Your only job is to grow your business

- The speed of a business is in direct relationship with the speed of its owner

- Failing to plan means planning to fail

- Your success is in direct relationship with the number of people who know you in a favourable light

- Ask yourself at least three times a day – am I being productive or just active?

- Ask for help. Don't abuse the help and always be ready to help others yourself

- Everything is negotiable

- Everything takes longer than you think and costs more than you think

Introduction

I have put one of these little sayings at the start of each chapter as a little reminder.

It is not hard to see that there are common factors running through businesses. Make money, make a product/service and survive. All of this while dealing with people issues, money issues and the law.

The law - what a simple word that is. Only three letters but how complex and rapidly changing those three letters are and how very serious the consequences of breaking them.

Business is an adventure. Have fun and avoid the pitfalls.

Chapter 1 - Make a list

Expect the unexpected

> *"The purpose of going into business is to expand beyond your existing horizons. So you can invent something that satisfies a need in the marketplace that has never been satisfied before. So you can live an expanded stimulating new life."*
>
> **The 7 Habits of Highly Effective People, Steven Covey**

When you start a new business there is a huge amount to do. This is still the case if you are buying an existing business or taking a franchise. You still have to deal with the fundamentals.

My first little tip

My first little tip is to buy and use a hard back book to act as your note pad, journal, phone list and general aide memoire. Pieces of paper and A4 pads get lost and used for other things. Have one book which is yours. I am pretty technological and have tried different types of planning software but I always come back to my book. It sits on my desk and I carry it home ready to use when I have an idea, to develop plans, to record meetings and telephone conversations. I always note the date against each entry. I didn't do this in my first ever book and found it a real drawback. Sometimes it is useful to be able to quote a date or to see exactly when something happened. It is especially good for passwords – non-sensitive ones of course!

Let me give you an example. Recently, I was having a planning session and I wanted some pricings for a web-based package I'd seen an advert for last year. When I first saw the ad, I rang the firm and had a chat with the sales team. Now, when I need it I can't remember the details of the product, who made it or the price. But when I telephoned the firm last year I noted all these details in my book. So, all I had to do was look in my book and there it all was.

And, as a bonus, you can look back through your books as time goes on and truly appreciate how your business has grown, how your thoughts and actions have changed and how your business has changed and developed.

Checklist

I thought it would be helpful at this early stage to give you as comprehensive a list as I can of the tasks involved in starting up a business. Some parts of the list won't apply to you depending on your business and it certainly won't cover everything for everyone – but it is a start.

My experience is there are some aspects which have to be in place before there is any point in doing anything else. I know it can be frustrating but you may just have to wait. A tempting offer on the price of letterhead is no good if you haven't decided your business name or address, or even phone number!

Remember, a word of warning: always expect the unexpected.

Here is a list of the things you have to organise before you can open your doors and take customers' money. This is effectively a list of subtitles. Each subtitle in practice will be broken down into smaller, specific tasks. Here's the list in no particular order. Sometimes life puts the list in order for you.

1. Decide on what your new business will do
2. Agree who you will start your business with
3. Make sure that all is OK at home with your family
4. Decide how much of your own money you want to/can invest
5. Decide a starting date
6. Decide a leaving date from your existing job
7. Research your market thoroughly
8. Draft a business plan
9. Decide which legal business structure suits you best
10. Decide how you will fund your business
11. Prepare your cash forecasts

12. Work out where your money will come from to live off in the early months
13. Open your bank accounts
14. Set up your trading structure
15. Advise the Revenue/VAT
16. Find premises if you need to
17. Raise the finance you need
18. Set up systems to manage your money on a day-to-day basis – do you need a bookkeeper?
19. Move into your premises
20. Set up your operations
21. Obtain the equipment you need
22. Employ the people you need
23. Put good Human Resources and Health & Safety practices in place
24. Decide how you will sell and go about your PR
25. Organise how customers will pay you
26. Who will handle your PAYE and VAT?
27. Set up your IT and websites
28. Sort out your tax and record keeping
29. Arrange your stationery eg letterhead etc
30. Arrange all the insurance you need
31. Deal with any professional registrations and restrictions
32. Deal with any particular legal registrations and restrictions

Due diligence

Whatever you are buying, always be careful. The seller may be trying to push or rush you. Don't be pushed or rushed. It's horrible to see clients who have spent money on a business relying on what they were told and then found later that it was at best hopeful and at worst fabricated. The courts will then be your only recourse. But litigation is very expensive in time and money. The judge will not be sympathetic to you if your only or best defence is that you relied on what you were told without checking adequately. The judge will inevitably take the view that you are an adult and so must have some share in your own misfortunes.

Buying an existing business

If you are buying an existing business you will still have to do a lot of the things in this list although there will probably be furniture, equipment, systems and people in place. You will though have a different set of tasks. There is no avoiding it, you must carry out full due diligence on the business before you agree to buy it. Don't ever rely on what you are told or on how things look. Even when you are spending a few grand on a second hand car, you look under the bonnet.

Make a list

Examine the accounts carefully, visit the premises as often as you can, talk to the employees and do some customer visits. Check any regulations that affect this industry, ask about and get details of past insurance claims and inspect all the licences the business has. Believe me, you can never do enough due diligence. At this stage, although money may be tight it is unbelievably important to get some good professional advice. Get your accountant to look over the figures and the information. They will look at the business dispassionately. They will see only the pictures painted by the figures. They will not have your burning desire to have this business and no other. Once you have handed your money over it is too late to find out that the sales figures are inadequate guesses at best and that the industry is collapsing. Always be prepared to walk away.

And what's more this level of due diligence is still important even if you are buying a business where you have worked or are working. I promise that there will be things you don't know. Get suspicious, this is your money, real money, you are spending.

> Here's an example in May 2010 when the new Government scrapped Home Information Packs (HIPS) overnight. Those businesses that had been created just to do HIPS were immediately out of business. If you had just bought a HIP

> company and you hadn't heard the rumblings that the new Government intended to scrap them you would have paid good money for absolutely nothing. Due diligence is vital.

Buying a franchise

If your new business involves the purchase of a franchise then once again you must be careful. Do your due diligence on the particular business you are interested in. Don't assume if you have looked closely at one franchise that they will be much the same. They won't be. Once again, it's your money and once you have parted with it it's very difficult to get it back. Look at the figures and satisfy yourself about the viability of the business model.

You can find out about franchises by reading franchise magazines or attending franchise business exhibitions. Please stay as objective as you can. Be sure that this is a business you can put your whole body and soul into for the next 10 years and make money.

The benefit of a franchised business is that most of the operating systems etc will already be in place. In theory you should simply only have to step into the model, work the model and make money. Think McDonald's.

But, as I said before, not all franchises are equal. Once again check the figures carefully. You will have to pay a substantial chunk of money to the franchisor to buy the franchise. A £10,000 purchase price is quite low. And again this is before you have taken a penny from your customers. You will then have to pay an annual fee to the franchisor, which is usually calculated as a percentage of your turnover for the whole period of the franchise agreement, which may be 10 years. Be sure you know how much support you will receive from the franchisor.

You should also consider whether your takings will earn back the lump sum you paid for the franchise quickly enough and be certain that you will be able to stomach the franchise fee that you will have to pay. Remember, that fee is often based on your turnover. I have heard many franchisees complain about the amount they pay. They feel resentful given the amount of hard work they have put into their business to have to give a chunk of their money away every year.

Over the years, I have often been asked to examine the terms of franchise agreements to see if the franchisee can get out of the agreement early. The common scenario is that the franchisee is happy to pay the initial capital purchase price because there is comfort in beginning a new business resting on the roots of an existing and successful business. The franchisee is happy with the initial price, with the annual fee and the term of the agreement. He is keen and eager.

As you would expect as the years go by the franchisee gains in experience and confidence. He feels resentful at paying every year and feels he gets nothing or very little back. The term of the agreement feels interminable. But almost always the franchise agreement is drawn up tightly and all the franchisee can do is to carry on until the end. He can then enter into another fresh agreement or come out of the agreement altogether. The problem then often arises that there may be a term in the agreement preventing him from setting up in competition! Definitely an issue.

Expect the unexpected

When you are starting up, always be prepared for the unexpected and for things to go wrong. As a solicitor's practice we are regulated by The Law Society and the Solicitors Regulation Authority (SRA). In order to start a new practice I had to obtain approval and registration through the SRA. I first had to have indemnity insurance in place and all this for a business which might never have started!

> In plenty of time, I received the appropriate registration form to begin in practice as a limited company from the SRA. I completed and returned it. The day before we were due to open I hadn't received my certificate. I rang the SRA and was told that I'd completed the wrong form. I pointed out that I'd completed the form I'd been sent by them! I went home that night planning to open up the next day and we didn't have SRA authorisation. Well, there was no point in worrying about it. The next morning at 9.00am I spoke to a senior lady in the SRA, explained all to her and received my authorisation. It could have been very bad indeed, but it wasn't.

Remember what I said at the start, expect the unexpected and everything takes longer than you think and costs more than you think.

In this chapter I have given you a very broad list of things which have to be done. Some of the tasks are quite straightforward and can be dealt with quite easily, others though need a bit of explanation. So the rest of this book will take you through some of those issues in more detail.

Chapter 2 - A crystal clear vision

Everything costs more than you think and takes longer than you think

You may have had a burning desire for years to run your own business or circumstances may have forced it upon you. Be very sure that it will suit your personality before you begin, as being an entrepreneur is not for everyone. Here is a blog post I received from Seth Godin, an internet marketer, which sounded a chord for me:

"You can see the determination in his eyes! That's the way a friend described someone she had just met. She was sure (just as I'm sure) that he's going places. Once the determination is in his eyes, the learning will take care of itself.

On the other hand, if I can see the fear in your eyes, then I'm not sure that learning alone will take care of the problem. No one can prove that the path you're on is risk free or guaranteed to work. Searching for more proof is futile. Searching for more determination makes more sense."

You know you want to start your own business. You are all fired up and excited but before you make the leap, invest time, create and write down a crystal clear vision of how you want your business to be. As Stephen Covey says "Begin with the end in mind."

Remember, if you don't know where you are going, any road will take you there. And as a bonus, by the time you have finished the crystal clear vision of your business it will feel so real you will feel extra excited and more than ready to get started.

When Tom Watson, the founder of IBM, was asked what he attributed the success of IBM to, he is quoted in the book *E-Myth Revisited* as answering:

> *"IBM is what it is today for three special reasons. The first reason is that, at the very beginning, I had a very clear picture of what the company would look like when it was finally done. You might say I had a model in my mind of what it would look like when the dream, my vision, was in place.*
>
> *The second reason was that once I had that picture I then asked myself how a company which looked like that would have to act. I then created a picture of how IBM would act when it was finally done.*
>
> *The third reason IBM has been so successful was that once I had a picture of how IBM would look when the dream was in place and how such a company would have to act, I then realised that, unless we began to act that way from the very beginning, we would never get there.*

> *In other words, I realised that for IBM to become a great company it would have to act like a great company long before it ever became one.*
>
> *From the very outset IBM was fashioned after the template of my vision. And each and every day we attempted to model the company after that template. At the end of each day, we asked ourselves how well we did, discovered the disparity between where we were and where we had committed ourselves to be and at the start of the following day set out to make up for the difference.*
>
> *Every day at IBM was a day devoted to business development – not doing business. We didn't do business at IBM, we built one."*

As we saw in the previous chapter, there are many practical things to do before you can start in business. It is immensely tempting to go ahead and do all the important, practical things and not give time and thought to planning. But it really is important to spend time envisioning your business in detail and working out a strategy for it. After all, you can't just sit behind your brand new desk on day one and expect customers to flock to you.

Even if you are starting your business with an existing client base you need to have thought through how all of it is going to work. You have to work out what you are selling and to whom and how. It's a bit dangerous to leave it all to the 20/20 vision you have with hindsight.

> One of my clients learned this the hard way. On the 1st March 2010 he started a lettings agency. He chose the name, designed a website and believed that his past experience would be enough to enable him to grow the business so that he could leave his day job, which he hated, before he was made redundant.
>
> After four months he had let a disappointing two houses and had one landlord on his books. He was facing losing his livelihood and the new business wasn't paying its way. He realised that he needed an identity for the business, a plan and a strategy. He sat in a darkened room and created his crystal clear vision for that new business. As a result he became more focused and more energised. The business began to grow and expand.

My crystal clear vision

Personally, I began to plan for my current solicitor's practice, The Law Practice (UK) Ltd, in June 2007 and it opened its doors in September 2007. I used those few months to become very clear about what sort of personality I wanted this new business to have.

After all it was my new baby and so it would have a character and personality all of its own. I spent time designing its appearance and character, doing its sums and working out where it was likely to be in terms of growth and development in two, three and four years. In retrospect, as with all new babies, its life has been affected by external forces out of my control but still it is growing and developing in line with my vision. Its core values, its personality, were developed in that early period and have provided a good stable framework against which to make decisions. If a decision does not fit with the personality of the firm, we simply do not take it.

I created a crystal clear vision of my business. I named the business, described the type of work it would do and for whom. I described in detail the offices from which the business would operate, how many people would work there, how many people would be employed in total and what each of them would do. I described the business systems, worked out and wrote down how many sales the business would do and how much money it would have.

It is worth saying at this stage that I have a mentor, a businessman who is very successful in his own right and who gives me no wriggle room whatsoever. I have his kind permission to mention his name as Gerard O'Donovan of Noble Manhattan Coaching Ltd. You will find his excellent company at 01305 769411 and www.noble-manhattan.com.

By the way, when you are in the early stages of setting up a business, I highly recommend you read *The Beermat Entrepreneur* by Mike Southon and Chris West; it's a down to earth and refreshingly practical book on how to start and run a business and then dispose of it. They make the point very clearly and in big letters that:

"A mentor is worth his or her weight in gold. They can be the difference between an idea's success and failure."

A mentor is often someone who is experienced in business, has lots of contacts and is willing to help you. Think *Dragons' Den* and you are on the right track!

Anyway, back to the crystal clear vision. The questions are reproduced here with my mentor's kind permission and I thank him. I found it extremely difficult to answer some of these questions at first but eventually I had thought about the business enough to know what it was, what it did, how it did it, how it was going to attract clients and the exact steps that were required of it to achieve its goals.

Be specific and realistic.

And then take action. Real positive, serious action.

Answering the questions I have written in this chapter will help you clarify exactly what it is you need to achieve in the business in order for it to grow and be profitable. It is very easy to get caught up in the hectic day-to-day, hurley burley of producing your product or service, finding and keeping customers and obtaining payment. Revisit your answers regularly. Check that you are still on track. If you are in business with a business partner then please do this exercise together as it is of vital importance that you are working from the same ethos and working towards the same goals.

> Here are the questions. I strongly recommend that you take time to answer them.
>
> 1. What is the unique business proposition for my customers? (This would be your elevator statement. By this I mean if you had one minute alone in a lift with any of the TV Dragons, what words would you use to explain exactly what your business is?)
>
> 2. What is the compelling business purpose for me and my team? (What is it you are all passionate about? What gets you into work every day?)
>
> 3. What are the goals for the business over the next two years?

4. Rewrite your two key goals in seven words or less beginning with an action word (ie establish, develop, agree, create etc).

5. What are the four key strategic breakthroughs you need in the next 12 months to achieve those two key goals?

6. What is the strategic breakthrough for each key goal it is critical to achieve in the first three months of your business?

7. To successfully implement your key goals, what are your key actions and by when?

8. Key actions

   Goal 1:   By when:

   Goal 2:   By when:

9. What is your action plan based on the above key actions and by when?

Elevator pitch

The first question is to identify the unique business proposition of your business. You may hear this referred to as the USP (Unique Selling Point). The idea is to develop a brief elevator pitch which would be enough to interest someone important in your business and keep them interested. Think Bill Gates is in a lift for 60 seconds and you just about have how long your elevator pitch should be. A well-honed sentence is perfect.
The unique business proposition of The Law Practice is to provide a range of legal services in a friendly, accessible way at a price that is reasonable and transparent. And briefly 'law with a friendly face.'

As your business develops you may find it useful to begin networking with other business people. You will find breakfast, lunchtime and evening groups of business people all gathered together to do business and expand their own networks. Most clubs charge an annual membership fee of between £250 and £500 and you have to pay for your food at each meeting, so you may be paying £10 a week.

Just Google business networking events and you will find lots in your area eg Business over Breakfast Clubs (BOB Clubs), BNI, Women in Business, and so on. At most of those meetings, you will have 60 seconds to make it clear to the group what your business is, who you are and what it is you want from that meeting. You must be clear, concise and above all memorable. You will be perhaps one of thirty or forty others. This is where a well-honed elevator pitch is invaluable. I have heard people deliver their 60 seconds and not even give their own name let alone the name of their business or what it does.

As a trainee solicitor many years ago, it was drummed into me:

"Stand up, speak up and shut up."

My own elevator pitch will depend upon what exactly I want to concentrate on at that particular meeting but it always contains the following words:

"Hello, my name is Gwyneth Allsopp. I am the Managing Director of The Law Practice. As a firm of solicitors we are different not in what we do but in the way that we do it… Thank you. That's Gwyneth Allsopp. The Law Practice – law with a friendly face."

The phrase "law with a friendly face" and our belief in that phrase actually informs everything that we do, create and design. There is a book called *Made to Stick* by Chip and Dan Heath that talks about the Commander's Intent. The concept is that in the military the

Commanding Officer receives a specific but not detailed order such as "Take the gun emplacement on the hill". His troops will then carry out that order in the best way possible given all the circumstances they find. But they will proceed with that intention only. Create with your elevator pitch your equivalent of the Commander's Intention. Measure all your decisions against it and don't take steps which deviate from the intention.

Always expect the unexpected

Remember things change. Any planning can only be done on the basis of things as they are now or as you anticipate them to be. The beauty and benefit of a small business is that it can be nimble and adapt to changes very quickly. *Be nimble and adapt to changes.*

Here's a bit more of my own story. As I have said, The Law Practice started in September 2007. Using actual and historic numbers I projected that about half of the cash would come from conveyancing work - that is people buying and selling houses. But quite suddenly, and without warning, in November 2007 the housing market crashed.

We went from 30 new conveyancing transactions a month to only seven. This was cataclysmic for our cash flow and meant that the plan had to be revisited. Now almost three years on, the numbers are only just starting to recover to those September 2007 levels. The effect on our cash flow and staffing requirements was immediate and serious. We made the necessary changes, pulled our belts in a bit tighter and actively began to seek other types of legal work. Necessity being the mother of invention and all that.

Chapter 3 - Writing a formal business plan

Failing to plan means planning to fail

It is essential to have a realistic, working business plan when you are starting up a business. A business plan is a written document that describes a business, its objectives, its strategies, the market it is in and its financial forecasts. It has many functions, from securing external funding to measuring success within your business. The business plan is a more formal and detailed version of your crystal clear vision. The vision turns into the plan. A business plan should be alive. It should be used. It's absolutely no use gathering dust in a drawer.

In the amazing book *E-Myth Revisited,* Michael Gerber at page 65 describes the job of the business owner as:

> *"Simply put your job is to prepare yourself and your business for growth. To educate yourself sufficiently so that, as your business grows, the business's foundation and structure can carry the additional weight.*
>
> *It's up to you to dictate your business's rate of growth as best you can by understanding the key processes that need to be performed, the key objectives that need to be achieved, the key position you are aiming your business to hold in the marketplace.*
>
> *Will you be wrong at times? Will you make mistakes? Will you change your mind? Of course you will! More often than not. But,*

done right, you will also have the contingency plans in place. Best case, worst case…

But all the while even while you're guessing, the key is to plan, envision and articulate what you see in the future both for yourself and your employees. Because if you don't articulate it, I mean write it down clearly so others can understand it, you don't own it.… Any plan is better than no plan."

Although at the start-up stage, creating a long and detailed business plan such as the one Tom Watson created for IBM may feel like a waste of time – you want to be out there in the cut and thrust of business – remember Mr Gerber's words "any plan is better than no plan".

If all you do is the crystal clear vision then that is a million times better than just opening up and trusting to luck.

A very successful client of mine who ran a profitable, large business always prepared a detailed, annual business plan, reviewed it quarterly at board meetings and redrafted it every year. You will need a reasonable business plan if you need to borrow money from the bank or to convince the bank manager that you need to maintain your current level of borrowings.

There is help

If all of this sounds daunting, don't panic, there are tools and people out there who can help you. Have a look in your local bookshop. There are a number of specialist books available that will help you draft a business plan.

Certainly at the time of writing most regions have a Business Link which are set up to assist business. All Business Links have people available as approved suppliers who are experienced in different aspects of business and who will help you create a business plan. There may even be some grant funding to help you pay for this assistance. This too can be accessed through, at the time of writing, your local Business Link. Just have a look at their website, there's a mine of really useful information: www.businesslink.gov.uk.

Personally, I have used a piece of software called Business Plan Pro, which provides a reasonably interactive way to put your business plan together. You have to buy the software and then work through its pre-set stages. There are a lot of standard plans on the software which are either useful templates or which maybe you can use with only a small amount of alteration. The site is www.paloalto.com. When I last looked the basic package was $99.95.

An accountant will often be able to help put your plan together although you may find that a bit costly. It is a useful alternative if you have an existing business which is perhaps struggling financially and so the plan needs to be sufficiently robust to satisfy an external financier.

I recommend a book called *Growing Your Business* by Gerard Burke, Liz Clarke, David Molian and Paul Barrow, which is written for owner/managers with the objective that if you read through the book and complete the assignments you will develop a detailed business plan that is practical and which works. At page five, the authors say:

> *"However most of the challenges that lie ahead for the growth hungry business are predictable. The remedies to managing these challenges require a degree of strategic thinking on the part of the owner/manager and a proactive approach to managing people, markets and money…*
>
> *For the owner/manager who takes time to anticipate and plan for challenges ahead the rewards can be great. The business can be easier to manage as it grows as well as being more profitable and more fun to run."*

There is also a useful Business Plan Wizard for creating a simple business plan on the website www.peterjones.tv of Peter Jones, the entrepreneur from *Dragons' Den*.

Generally, a business plan will include:

- **An index listing the contents of the business plan**

- **An executive summary**

    The executive summary is a synopsis of the key points of your entire plan. It should include highlights from each section of the rest of the document – from the key features of the business opportunity through to the elements of the financial forecasts. Its purpose is to explain the basics of your business in a way that both informs and interests the reader. If, after reading the executive summary, an investor or manager understands what the business is about and is keen to know more, it has done its job.

- **Your background**

    Add into the plan details of your experience and CV. Detail how much money and time you have already invested and how much more of both you are prepared to invest.

- **Your people**

  Begin with your management team, if there is one. Describe their backgrounds, experience and roles in the business individually and with a brief CV for each member of the team. Describe how much they have invested so far in time and money and how much more are they prepared to invest. Explain what their anticipated salaries will be with bonuses etc. This part of the plan should identify the strengths in your team and your plans to deal with any obvious weaknesses.

  Give details of your workforce in terms of total numbers and by department. Spell out what work you plan to do internally and if you plan to outsource any work. Your plan should also outline any recruitment or training plans, including timescales and costs.

- **Market analysis**

  Describe in detail what you are going to sell, where and to whom. Back this up with statistics wherever possible. Who will your main customer(s) be? Show that you have researched the possible markets for your product or service, that you are aware of the difficulties and the opportunities and the likely timescales. Remember your competitors. It is important to know your competitors' strengths and weaknesses as compared to your own and it is a good idea to do a competitor analysis of each one.

- **Sales**

   Describe how you are going to reach your target market in order to sell to them. What is your sales pitch? How are you actually going to sell? Will you use telesales, mailshots, the internet, networking, referrals or a mixture of all of these and how much will these all cost? A networking group can cost a membership of £500 per year plus VAT and the weekly meeting fee of £10.

   This section should describe the specific activities you intend to use to promote and sell your products and services. Think about your pricing policy. Will it differentiate between customers or products?

- **Your operations**

  Your business plan also needs to outline your operational capabilities and any planned improvements. How you actually produce your goods and services will be very dependent upon the nature of your business. For example mine is fairly people intensive but I decided we didn't need a traditional shop front premises. We moved into a suite of offices and immediately saved the cost of a receptionist.

  Think about whether you will need any investment. If you do the work, are paid straight away and have 30 to 60 days in which to pay your suppliers you almost certainly won't need a bank overdraft. This is the time to consider whether you will need any premises and if so where they ideally should be situated, how big they need to be and whether you want to lease or not and for how long. I worried long and hard over entering into a five year lease for the offices we use now.

  Give some thought to all of your systems. You will need everyone working the same way and the only way to achieve this is with written and computerised systems. You must also think about how you will manage growth, but with everything electronic comes a cost. Plan and budget for this as much as you can.

- **Forecasts**

    Prepare detailed financial forecasts, which show your cash projections, sales forecasts and profit and loss. As part of your plan you will need to provide a set of financial projections that translate what you have said about your business into numbers. These forecasts give an idea as accurately as you can at this time of how much capital you need if you are seeking external funding, the security you can offer lenders, how you plan to repay any borrowings and sources of revenue and income.

    I do appreciate it is very difficult to do and we are always very optimistic when we prepare our forecasts but your forecasts should run for the next three or even five years. However, the first 12 months' forecasts should have the most detail associated with them. Include the assumptions behind your projection with your figures, both in terms of costs and revenues so investors can clearly see the thinking behind the numbers.

- **Action plan**

    Specify everything you are going to do in the first 30 days. Then specify your actions into a 100 day plan. The strategic planning you have already done will help you with this.

Chapter 4 - Cash: borrow safely

Have you ever heard of a business failing because it had too much money?

Cash flow forecasting

I am one of those really sad people who come back from holiday and the first question I ask is "How's the cash doing?" Believe me I've learned the hard way that cash is the life blood of any business. Without it everything is just too hard. But it's really easy when you are in the cut and thrust of business to forget to monitor the cash. Even worse, it can be psychologically impossible to bring yourself to look at your business bank balance when you know it looks bad. After all, nobody likes bad news. And the real problem is that once your cash has tightened up or frozen up, which is far worse, it can often be too late to do anything about it.

The very best way to finance your young business is through revenue – its own cash. By that I mean through the money the business creates itself. This is far better than any form of external funding. You do this by keeping the sales flowing in, keeping the customers paying on time and keeping outgoings as low as possible.

It is vital that every business should maintain a cash flow forecast that is as accurate as possible. After all, have you ever known a business go bust because it had too much money?

An accurate cash flow forecast will allow you to predict, with reasonable accuracy, peaks and troughs in your available cash. You know how much cash you have received and what you anticipate your outgoings to be. You can project that into the future. You will see at a glance when, or if, you are going to exceed your overdraft. You will see immediately that you need more work. You will appreciate that you need to reduce your costs.

Be careful of false economies though. It's a fine line to tread between spending money on things you don't actually need and can do without and not spending it on staying up to date, or being fully trained or not having a good website. It's a really good discipline for me to put together a case for any purchase to my cashier who is very sceptical. After all, she's the one who handles the bank and the payments all the time. Cash is very real to her. If she isn't convinced we simply don't buy it.

I have created my own cash flow forecast in Excel and I update it at least weekly. By forecasting my own cash I realised very early on that on my business's first birthday there would be a lot of bills to pay. Just think, a year from when you first start you have to pay for your insurances, membership renewals, software licence renewals, annual lease and licence fees.

Ideally you should create your cash flow forecast in the months before you start to trade. You have no real idea of how much anything is going to cost, how much work you are going to receive or what your cash flow will look like. The best you can do is to create a best estimate. I have looked at a lot of cash flow forecasts and understand that naturally you will be overly optimistic about your sales and cash receipts and not realistic enough about your expenditure.

As the months go by you will gradually start to acquire real, actual figures which you can put into the cash forecast and which will help to make the forecast more accurate. But remember what happened to us with the conveyancing work. I put figures into my cash flow forecast that reflected the actual work we had received and then suddenly it disappeared. My cash flow forecast was seriously wrong. I had to make the necessary adjustments urgently.

One of the things that I have learned in my business life is that everything takes longer than you think and costs more than you think. This is one of the reasons that experienced business people advise that you get to know your figures and that you check where you are against them every day or half day. You've got time then to put things right. If you rely on your management accounts, which may only be produced monthly, or the end of year accounts from the accountant, you are working with historical figures.

By the time you see the figures the damage is done and has been compounded many times over.

When preparing the business cash flow forecast you must estimate what your own financial needs are, especially if you have left your day job and this business is your only source of income. You will need to calculate your personal living costs so that you can budget a salary for yourself which will cover your personal expenses. One of the best tips I can give you is to pay yourself a salary from the business. You may well find that you are paid less than your employees but you must be paid.

I know a solicitor with a small business who doesn't pay herself any salary whatsoever. Truly I don't know where she finds the motivation to get up and do it every day! It is very difficult to remain motivated and deal with the stresses and long hours of a new business if you are not receiving any financial reward from it at all.

Surely it is better to go and work for somebody else. At least your mortgage will be paid.

Have a look at the following list, it may help you to think about your personal expenses:

Approximate cost per month	
Rent/mortgage	£
Heating, lighting	£
Rates, water rates	£
Food for the family	£
Clothing for the family	£
Credit card/loan repayments	£
Entertainment including TV & satellite	£
Car finance	£
Petrol, running costs, insurance	£
All the other items	£
Subtotal	£
ADD 10% for emergencies	£
TOTAL	£ per month

Keep this total figure as low as possible and then put it into your cash flow forecast. This is the amount you need every month just to live. This has to be the minimum for your salary.

My own mentor's words of wisdom to me when I first started were:

- To spend as little as I sensibly can on anything I buy
- To count the cost of everything
- That everything I buy, and I do mean everything, is negotiable
- To wait and see. Have you ever had the idea in your mind that you really need something for yourself or the business? You just can't wait and you go out and buy it. Then you find that you don't use it or you already have something similar that will do the same thing.

Stationery is a good example of this. For some reason, stationery is addictive. There are very few businesses who don't have a stocked stationery cupboard – and if they are honest, an overstocked one.

The lure of half price envelopes and letter heads is hard to resist. My own business has operated for almost three years using up the stationery in its cupboards left by the old firm!

Capital expenditure

It is unavoidable that there will be some capital items you would struggle to do without, although, believe me, there will be fewer than you think if you are a bit cautious. Remember everything you buy represents money out of your precious start-up pot.

The sorts of things that you may have to buy in these early days are computers, printers, a fax machine, filing cabinets, desks and desk chairs, a telephone system or mobiles and stationery. You will always save money if you can buy equipment second hand. It is very tempting when you are starting your beautiful new business to furnish it with beautiful new furniture. Restrain yourself. There is absolutely no point, as a client of mine did, in spending £35,000 on a new, incredibly sophisticated till system for his shop when a tin cash box with a key would have done.

Agree with yourself that you will shop around to buy the cheapest, best equipment that you can find. Give yourself a budget and stick to it. Spread the payment over as long as possible, always being mindful of the interest you may be paying. Interest free credit cards are wonderful to cover these early start-up costs but just keep an eye on them because that attractive deal only stays attractive while you are meeting the minimum monthly payments. I absolutely promise that you will forget to set up a monthly bank payment and so you will forget to make a payment one month causing the interest rate to soar.

Somewhere in your area there will be a second-hand office furniture supplier where you will be able to buy attractive good quality but cheap office furniture. It's pretty good fun to prowl around these places just to see what is there and what bargains you can pick up. You can always replace your second hand stuff once you have money in your business bank account – if you can bring yourself to spend that hard-earned cash on filing cabinets at that stage!

Please don't do what I did – I listened to OTHER PEOPLE in respect to one particular buying decision. I asked people in my new team about numbers because numbers affected the cost of the thing I was buying. They gave me numbers which were massively wrong and I am ashamed to say I didn't check or – I am sorry to say – stop to think. I went ahead and entered into a contract with a supplier at a cost of £400 per month because that was the cost based on the numbers I had been given. As the months went by it became very clear that the numbers were 10, maybe 100, times exaggerated.

I terminated that agreement as soon as I could.

One of your earlier decisions will be where to locate your business. I talk about this in much more detail later. The cheapest option is to work from home but sometimes this is neither attractive nor possible. Your alternative will be to enter into a formal lease that will provide you with the space you need at an agreed rent for an agreed period.

If you just need office space, consider serviced offices. With these you will usually pay monthly for the actual square footage you rent from them. You get flexibility to suit the needs of your business. If you need more space you pay more and if you need less or to move out altogether you just have to give a month's notice. Often included in the rent is a receptionist who will answer your telephones, organise meeting rooms and in some cases arrange tea and coffee.

Cash: borrow safely

Premises expenses

Running your office will give you another set of monthly expenses. As with your personal living costs, estimate these as accurately as you can and add those estimated figures into your cash flow forecast:

Approximate figures per month	
Rent	£
Rates, water rates	£
Electricity, heating etc	£
Telephones (rental and bills)	£
Postage	£
Insurances	£
Cleaning	£
Printing	£
Advertising, sales, marketing	£
Accountancy fees	£
Legal fees	£
Training fees	£
Trade organisation membership	£
Bookkeeping/wages	£

Loan repayments	£	
Credit card repayments	£	
Sundry items	£	
Salaries (including yours)	£	
PAYE	£	
TOTAL	£	per month

AND always add a bit. There is always something unforeseen.

This total figure is your business overhead.

If you are earning enough every month to cover your overhead then your bank balance will stay pretty much in credit. If you don't earn enough to cover your overhead, you use up the cash in the bank and overdraft. You are broke and you no longer have a business. When you hear of firms cutting costs it is these costs that they are cutting. Just imagine, it is perfectly possible by losing one employee to save £2,000 a month or £24,000 a year. A lot of money.

If your business is likely to manufacture products or sell on by retail then these figures become more complicated. You will have to add to these figures the cost of the raw materials you are using to manufacture the products, which you are then going to sell or the wholesale cost of the goods that you have to buy to put into your shop.

Chapter 5 - To limit or not to limit

The speed of the business is in direct relationship with the speed of the owner

One of the decisions you will have to make very early in your business planning is what sort of legal vehicle your business will use. There are a number of different ways that you can run a business and each has different legal, financial and tax consequences.

Your options

Often the simplest and cheapest way to start-up in business is under your own name or under a business name as a sole trader. My first business was called Allsopp Solicitors. The drawback is if there are any problems, such as bad debts, these will be personal to you. It will be you personally who will be open to be sued in the courts or tribunals for non-payment of debts, commercial or other disputes. Any County Court Judgement (CCJ) will affect you personally and not the business.

All contracts, for example for the purchase of goods, your lease and employment contracts, will be in your sole name as will any bank loan or overdraft. The biggest single threat you will face as a sole trader is the loss of your house if you are sued successfully or if you give a personal guarantee to secure a debt (more about personal guarantees later). If you do set up in business as a sole trader (or really at all) you must advise Her Majesty's Revenue and Customs (HMRC) who now deal with income tax, national insurance and VAT. For this you can call 08459 154515.

However you finally choose to operate, the choice of your business name is very important. I talk later about the legal and regulatory constraints in registering a company name but just be certain about the name you select. It will be with you for as long as you are in business as changing it can be expensive and sometimes damaging. A big institution such as Norwich Union will not have taken the decision to change its name to Aviva lightly.

Your name needs to be memorable but not offensive. It needs to sum up what you do. This is why I was particularly pleased to be able to register The Law Practice (UK) Ltd. It sums up what we do very explicitly. I also have a related business named My Business Lawyer, which again does what it says on the tin. If you are a therapist, a plumber, a florist, an optician, a coach – say so.

If you plan to start your new business with other people or once you have started you decide to take a partner into the business, then clearly you can't carry on in business as a sole trader.

You will have to consider the other options, which are:

- Partnership
- Limited Liability Partnership (LLP)
- Limited company (Ltd)
- Public limited company (Plc)
- Company limited by guarantee
- Charity

In my experience most new businesses start life as a sole trader, a partnership or a limited company, although it is always possible to start your business in one way and then as it grows and develops change how you trade. Often the bank or your accountant will advise you about changing from say a partnership to a limited company. The decision is always yours but do take notice.

You will need some accountancy advice though if you want to do that as HMRC treats each entity differently and you need to phase the change as carefully as you can to maximise any tax advantages and minimise tax risks. You really don't want to be facing a double tax bill. Remember the cash.

Circumstances may dictate how you trade. Someimes you won't even be considered for a Local Authority or an NHS Trust contract unless you trade as a limited company.

Partnership

If you plan to start your business with other people then consider a partnership. A partnership is again a cheap and simple way to begin in business. Partnerships can have the same sorts of benefits as a company (they are called LLP – Limited Liability Partnerships) but as most partnerships are not limited, the partners are open to the same sorts of liabilities that the sole trader faces. The legal and taxation consequences are pretty much the same as if you are a sole trader.

Also, there is a weird concept in partnership, which is that the partners have joint and several liability for any contracts they enter into. This means that either or both are liable for the whole amount of the sum owed. If one partner has more cash or assets then an astute creditor will pursue that partner first in the expectation of receiving payment in full from them.

The legal relationships between partners themselves and then between the partnership and the outside world are mainly defined in the Partnership Act 1909. There is more recent legislation such as the Partnership Act 1980 and then the Limited Liability Partnership Act 2007 but in default of a written agreement between the partners, the terms of the 1909 Act will be applied. And as a matter of interest that Act defines a partnership as "…the relationship between persons carrying on a business in common with a view to profit".

I had this exact discussion with a client recently. He had traded at a reasonable level as a sole trader for a number of years and felt that he needed to incorporate – become a limited company. We looked at his business in some detail. Effectively, he repaired and serviced pieces of scientific equipment in schools.

He had full insurance cover just in case anything went wrong and his private finances were modest. He did not own a house, so if anything went that badly wrong, he did not have a lot to lose, which I appreciate is Dutch comfort. I advised him that he did not have enough risk to justify the cost and the increased regulation he would have had as a limited company. He was a bit concerned though that he would inherit quite a lot of money in the future so he would then have something to lose. We agreed that when that happened that would be a good time to incorporate.

Limited company

Another alternative way for the business to operate is as a limited company. In law, the company is a separate legal entity (person) from its directors or shareholders so if the company enters into a contract or gets into trouble, it is the company, usually, which is sued and not the people. However, the directors remain vulnerable as individuals if they sign a personal guarantee on behalf of the company or act outside their powers as directors. Also they can face disqualification from being directors and criminal proceedings if they allow the company to continue to trade while knowing it is insolvent or the company commits acts or omissions of negligence which result in death, such as serious railway accidents.

Be very careful, though, if you do plan to start in business with other people, either in partnership or as directors of a company. I talk at some length about this in my book *The People in your Business*. I absolutely promise that there will be tensions, jealousies and resentments. Most of the people whom I see before they start up their new business are doing so from the springboard of another business where they are in partnership. The relationships in the partnership have soured to such a degree that it has to break up.

Limited company checklist

Here is a checklist to help you set up and register your limited company to make sure that it is on a proper legal footing before it starts in business. Make sure you:

- Display your company's name clearly on all of its business stationery including letters, invoices, receipts and cheques.

- Show your company's place of registration, registered number and registered office address on its business letters, order forms, e-mails and faxes.

- If you have a company website show the company's name, registered office and geographic addresses, registered company number, VAT number and your e-mail address.

- Display your company's name clearly on the outside of its offices or other places of business.

- If any of the company directors' names are included in letters other than in the text of the letter or as the name of the person signing the letter you must include the names of all of the directors.

- Send all of the necessary registration documents and forms to the Registrar of Companies completed and signed.

- Appoint an accountant to prepare your company accounts for filing at Companies House at the end of each trading year.
- The company comes into existence when the Registrar of Companies issues a Certificate of Incorporation. Be sure that you receive your certificate and that it is correct.

- Contact HM Revenue and Customs to register your new company with them.

Companies House provides a lot of useful information which you will find at www.companieshouse.gov.uk. Its enquiry telephone number is 0303 1234 500. There is also useful information on starting up and running a small business on www.businesslink.gov.uk.

A company can be a very tiny business. The legal requirement is that a private company must have at least one director who must be an actual person. It is not essential to have a company secretary. This sort of company is called a 'single member' private company for which there are special rules that can be found on the Companies House website. If there is only one director this must be stated in one of the company's official documents called its Articles of Association.

Risk

Whichever of these identities you choose will largely depend upon how much personal, financial and legal risk you and your life and business partners are comfortable being exposed to. Please remember that your business decisions will affect whoever you share your life with at home. If a decision goes badly wrong then it is your life partner's home that is at risk as well as your own.

A client of mine recently lost his business. It went into liquidation and took all of his personal money with it as he had used his own money to prop the business up. His wife therefore had to support him and the family until he could find a job. Their savings had all but gone so she had to work full-time rather than part-time and to make matters worse, she had signed a lease agreement as guarantor for the business, so she was personally responsible for that debt even though she had no involvement in the business whatsoever.

If you are, for example, starting an internet based networking business there is not likely to be much risk to you and so you could safely begin as a sole trader or as a partnership. However, if you have to enter into large, valuable contracts, make large purchases or take a lease for premises then limited liability would be a much better option.

Personal guarantees

By signing a personal guarantee an individual is accepting that they will be responsible for the payment of the debt whether or not their company is in a position to pay. Do you remember when we talked about the protection that individuals receive when they trade in business as a limited company? If the company has financial difficulties the directors of the company will not be personally affected by them unless they have made themselves personally liable for any of the company's debts or contracts. The classic way that a director will do this is by signing a personal guarantee.

I've seen so much distress caused by personal guarantees over the years that they've become a hobby horse of mine. If you need an overdraft for your business or if you are buying or leasing a piece of equipment you may be asked for personal guarantees. In one word, don't. BEWARE. If you are asked for a personal guarantee please take advice, refuse to give one and shop around. If the guarantee is called in, it will almost certainly cost you a lot of money or your home.

I was amazed recently to be asked by someone who had been in business for many years as the director of a limited company whether their house was at risk if they gave the bank a personal guarantee. The answer clearly, definitely and emphatically is YES.

The actual practical consequences of this are that if the company gets into financial difficulties and has a loan or an overdraft with the bank, which is secured by a personal guarantee from one or more of the directors then the bank can, and will, collect the debt from those directors.

The bank will write to the personal guarantor requesting payment, can close down that person's private banking facility with the bank, can begin county court proceedings against the guarantor and can obtain a charge against the guarantor's house. If the debt can't be repaid, in whole or in part, then the bank can take possession of the guarantor's home to sell it to repay the debt. The bank can and will obtain a CCJ against the guarantor, which will affect that person's credit rating and in some circumstances the bank will take personal bankruptcy proceedings.

I have known banks and other businesses take enforcement action of this sort as long as two years after the company has got into financial difficulty and ceased trading. A retired couple came to see me recently. They were being harassed and hounded by debt collectors on behalf of a major high street bank to recover £10,000 owed under a personal guarantee. The story was that the couple had owned an engineering company with an unsecured overdraft with this bank of £20,000. They needed to increase that limit temporarily during 2006 to £40,000. They signed personal guarantees to the bank to protect all money owed to the bank by them at any time. Within three months the overdraft was returned to £20,000.

In 2010 the company ceased trading. However, the couple began to be pursued by these debt collectors under these personal guarantees for £10,000. They had not appreciated and it was not explained to them that the guarantees were not cancelled when the overdraft limit was reduced back to £20,000. It stayed in place to protect all money owed to the bank.

Lenders are much more likely to request personal guarantees if they are being asked to provide finance to a limited company. If the business is a sole trader or a partnership the bank is effectively providing the finance to the individuals in that business and so the individuals will be pursued for payment just in the same way as if a director had given a personal guarantee.

So, the lesson is, personal guarantees are very serious and should be avoided at all costs. Walk away from the deal rather than give one.
When I was setting up The Law Practice I received identical terms from two high street banks who wanted my account. The only difference between them was that one bank required a personal guarantee from me to protect the overdraft and the other did not. By

now it probably wouldn't surprise you that I chose the bank that did not want a guarantee.

Interestingly, when I told the other bank of my choice and my reasons my account enquiry was referred to a more senior manager and HEY PRESTO I was offered exactly the same banking terms but without the personal guarantee! You might just want to know that I went with the first bank anyway because I had so much to do in those few short weeks that I needed to get some of them crossed off my list. The decision was made for me and I stuck by it.

Business name

You need to be careful when you choose your business name, whether you trade with just a trading name or as a limited company. You may well be warned off by solicitors if you choose a name that is too similar or the same as an existing and possibly well-known business name. I have acted more than once for businesses that have received letters from solicitors threatening an injunction and other serious court action unless they changed their name because their name was too similar to that of another large and well-known company. Large firms who have spent years and millions of pounds in raising their brand image often do not take too kindly to their names being copied. In these circumstances you don't have too much choice but to comply. They usually have much deeper pockets than you. You will have to change your name, register the new name and change your stationery etc.

If you want to trade as a company, checking name availability is easy by using the Companies House website at www.companieshouse.gov.uk. Select the free Webcheck service on that site and enter the possible names you want to see if they are already being used. When I did this there was another Law Practice Ltd but I was able to register The Law Practice (UK) Ltd as it is sufficiently different to be accepted. The general principle is that you cannot choose a name that is the same as that of a company which already exists. You should avoid names that people may find offensive, sensitive names and names that are potentially misleading for example using words such as international if you are a UK-only business.

> Just a little tip; you can register your limited company direct at Companies House or you can use the services of a company formation agent, accountant or solicitor who will do it for you. Companies House charges a standard registration fee of £20 and also offers a same-day registration service for a fee of £50. A search on the internet for Companies House will also bring up a number of paid adverts for company formation agents who offer a range of services for a range of prices from between £25 to £500.

Chapter 6 - Leave your present job!

Your success is in direct relationship with the number of people who know you in a favourable light

Almost as a necessity some time after you start your new business, you will have to leave your old job. Over the years the stories I have heard about this stage are as varied as there are people on the planet. Each case is different because the people, the business, the relationships and the finances are all different. One thing remains the same though – you are creating change and that is stressful for everyone involved.

When I began The Law Practice (UK) Ltd it was with the blessing of my old firm. We took over a branch office of theirs together with the staff, office and computers. All was happy and amicable for some months and then for some indefinable reason the relationship changed and began to cool. Fortunately it didn't matter – but it could have.

One of the nastiest pieces of court litigation I have ever advised upon involved four men who left their employment, set up in business and then were served with court injunctions by their previous employer who was seeking to stop them using the employer's confidential information in their new business and to close the business down because it was in direct competition. The dispute was eventually settled by agreement after some months but not until it had delayed the start of the new business, taken the new owners' eye off the ball and cost thousands in fees.

So it's important to get it right and I would always advise you to be as open and transparent as you can. Tell your employer or fellow business owners what it is you plan to do and where. And this is particularly important if you are a senior member of staff with a lot of knowledge and contacts. Communicate.

We need to look at what can happen if you are an employee and then if you are already in business with others.

Terminating your employment contract

If you are an employee and want to start in business on your own, you must look carefully at the terms of your employment contract before you take any action. Most employment contracts, especially for senior people, managers and directors will contain some form of restrictive covenant. You may have heard these referred to as restraint of trade clauses.

A restrictive covenant is a term in the employment contract which seeks to prohibit you from competing with your ex-employer either in your own right or as part of another business, or seeks to prevent you from soliciting customers of the ex-employer by using knowledge of those customers gained during their prior employment. It will also seek to protect the ex-employer's confidential documents, information and staff.

So the sort of terms to look for in your own employment contract will look a bit like these, although clearly the exact wording will be different.

Here is an example of a non-competition clause:

"The employee hereby agrees not to:

1) directly or indirectly compete with the business of the company and its associated companies during the period of employment and for a period of one year following termination of employment and notwithstanding the cause or reason for termination; and

2) for a period of one year following termination of employment; directly or indirectly, whether on his/her own behalf or in conjunction with any person, company, business entity or other organisation whatsoever, solicit, assist in soliciting, accept, or facilitate the acceptance of, or deal with, in competition with the company, the custom or business of any customer or prospective customer with whom he/she has had substantial

personal contact or dealings on behalf of the company during the period of employment.

This non-competition agreement shall extend only for a radius of 10 miles from the present location of the company. The term 'not compete' as used herein shall mean that the employee shall not own, manage, operate, consult or be employed in a business substantially similar to or competitive with, the present business of the company or such other business activity in which the company may substantially engage during the term of employment."

Here is an example of a non-solicitation clause:

"The employee agrees not to for a period of six months immediately following the termination of employment, either on his/her own account or in conjunction with or on behalf of any other person, company, business entity or other organisation whatsoever, directly or indirectly solicit the custom or business of any customer or prospective customer of the company with whom he/she has had substantial personal contact or dealings on behalf of the company during the period of employment."

And a non-poaching clause:

"The employee agrees not to for a period of six months immediately following the termination of employment, either on his/her own account or in conjunction with or on behalf of any other person, company, business entity or other organisation whatsoever, directly or indirectly induce, solicit, entice or procure, any person who is a company employee to leave such employment, where that person is a company employee on the termination date; or accept into employment or otherwise engage or use the services of any person who is a company employee on the termination date; or had been a company employee in any part of the three months immediately preceding the termination date."

It is important to note though that these covenants which seek to restrict the activities of an employee after his employment has ended are considered at first sight to be unenforceable against the employee because they are against general public policy. The extent of the clauses must be relative to the employee's position within the business. More senior employees will be in contact with more sensitive information and so more onerous restrictions may be placed upon them.

The courts will consider the validity of such clauses against the background of each set of facts. The employer will be successful if he can convince the court that the covenant is designed to protect his legitimate business interests and that it extends no further than is reasonably necessary to protect those interests. The court can delete some parts of a clause if the remaining parts make independent sense without the need to change the wording and the sense of the contract is not changed. If the employer is successful, the court will uphold the term and will allow the covenant to be enforced.

I know that I have become very legal in this section but this is very important. If you have one of these terms, if you breach it and that causes your ex-employer any financial loss you could be facing a very large bill indeed. You will be stopped from trading and you will have legal bills to pay.

If an employer has reason to believe that an employee has breached a restriction the most common remedy sought is an injunction. An application will generally be made for an interlocutory injunction pending full trial. This means that the court will be asked to stop you immediately on an emergency basis. The court will have the briefest of information to make this decision and you won't know about it at all until you receive the injunction order served upon you personally by a process server. Not pleasant believe me.

You may be able to head off any further court hearings if you can make an agreement with the ex-employer. This could mean that you agree not to use any confidential information or that you will not open your new business when and where you planned. If you don't reach an agreement the whole dispute goes back to the court. The court hears the evidence of both sides and will make a decision.

Terminating a business partnership

Many people come to see me to get advice as to how they can safely get out of their existing business so that they can start on their own. These are people who are already in a partnership or are directors in a company. The motivation is often that they are not happy where they are, they may feel resentful that they are doing more than the other owner(s) or they simply feel restricted or unhappy about the direction in which their business is going.

This whole situation is often made worse because the people left behind are often your friends or family members. You may have set that business up together and now you feel guilty about wanting to leave. On a personal note it is better to leave while you still feel guilty and before you feel resentful.

A couple of stories come to mind. The first involved two ladies who set up a courier business together and ran it quite comfortably for a few years. Without any prior warning one of them announced that she was leaving the business, then, that day. Not only was that a shock which created all sorts of organisational issues, but she also emptied the partnership bank account.

The second involved two business partners running a company which had been originated by the father of one of them. The son of the original owner felt that he was the senior of the two partners. Meanwhile the second partner believed he did all the work while the other took all the credit and the money. A recipe for disaster and resentment all round.

When you are planning to leave an existing business you must check whatever agreements you put in place either when you started the business or when you joined. You are looking for the sorts of clauses we considered in some detail relating to employees as these clauses may be in a partnership agreement, director's employment contract or shareholders' agreement.

If there are no terms restricting you then you can do largely what you want provided you do not breach your implied duties as a director of a company to act in the best interests of the company. But I have learned that what goes around comes around. By all means decide what your new business will do, where it will be and with whom but just stop to consider if that will impact on your old business in any way. If it does and if you can talk it through with your existing business partners, try to reach an agreement.

What I learned when we took over the old firm's branch office is that you think the new business will start afresh and cut the ties but no, for at least three years, albeit on a diminishing basis, we have had contact with the old firm. The relationship stayed pretty reasonable and so we have been able to work together to resolve these client issues. It would have been very difficult verging on impossible if the relationship had soured.

So when you leave to start up be careful that you aren't too openly and directly in competition, don't poach their staff and don't use their confidential information to your commercial advantage.

A couple of my clients have done this over the past months. One dreaded the conversation and it turned out OK as he was prepared to be very reasonable. He agreed with the old firm which clients he would take with him and how his pipeline fees would be paid and when. The other was put on garden leave for three months so that he couldn't contact his clients in that time and has then been left to run his business as he wishes. There is no restriction on him now that the three month period has expired.

Garden leave

I have mentioned garden leave so I'd better explain what it is. Garden leave allows an employer to require an employee to spend all or part of the notice of termination period at home while continuing to receive his usual salary and benefits. The employee cannot take up other employment and is no longer privy to the company's confidential information. Many contracts for senior people contain a clause allowing garden leave. If it is not in the contract the parties can agree to it as a sensible solution to this issue. It is also commonly used in conjunction with restrictive covenants. A person should only be placed on garden leave for a reasonable period of time. But as one of my client's has done recently you could use the period of garden leave to do the necessary organisation to set up not one but two businesses!

Liabilities

And, lest I forget, when you leave an existing business it is vital that you make sure you are released from any financial or legal liabilities that you entered into on behalf of the business.

What do I mean? Well you may have entered into a lease for property or equipment on behalf of the company. You may have given a personal guarantee to the bank or allowed your home to be used as security against business bank borrowing or a factoring arrangement. These arrangements will not automatically end just because you are no longer in that business. They will move with you. You must actively terminate each agreement and be formally released from the obligation. Beware though that this may cause problems for the remaining business owners who have to either replace your security or try to convince the lender or provider that even without you the money or equipment is secure.

Notice

If you are an employee your employment contract will tell you how much notice you should give your employer. If you don't have a contract then there are statutory minimum periods of notice.

The minimum legal notice period to be given by an employer is:

- One week's notice if the employee has been employed by the employer continuously for one month or more, but for less than two years

- Two weeks' notice if the employee has been employed by the employer continuously for two years, and one additional week's notice for each further complete year of continuous employment, up to a maximum of 12 weeks.

The minimum statutory notice period which must be given by an employee is at least one week's notice if employed continuously for one month or more by that employer. Note that the maximum notice period is 12 weeks after 12 or more years' continuous service.

Minimum notice does not apply if you are an independent contractor or freelance agent and employees whose fixed-term contracts have come to an end, with a few exceptions.

These minimum periods are often extended in written contracts of employment.

If you are a business owner then you probably won't have a contract and so the amount of notice you give should be reasonable in all circumstances. It can be a hard decision between allowing you to leave or forcing you to stay when you are far from motivated with your mind and heart elsewhere. Also, you continue to have access to the business's confidential information, but this has to be balanced with the disruption that your sudden departure could cause.

Personally, on balance I believe that if someone is leaving they should go as soon as possible. I have heard of very senior people being made to work a full six months' notice. My preference is to let someone go as soon as they tell me they wish to resign. I will either pay in lieu of notice or put the person on garden leave so they are out of the way and can't cause any damage.

Chapter 7 - What is our address?

Everything is negotiable

Deciding on and then finding the best premises and location for your business can often be a difficult and time-consuming problem. And to make matters worse getting this decision right can vary in importance from nil to absolutely crucial. Much will depend on the type of business you plan to start, the amount and type of accommodation you need, where your customers are, the requirements of your personal life and the clients or customers you plan to serve.

Sometimes you have little choice. After all, if you plan to run a shop you need to find shop premises. The only decisions left to make are where and how much.

I moved my business during its first six months. We were in traditional solicitors' offices with a shop window, a reception and a receptionist. I asked the receptionist to log the number of people who actually called in and why they came. After a couple of weeks of this it was apparent that we didn't need the shop front, the reception or the receptionist. So we moved into an office block and I saved the salary for the receptionist immediately.

Over the years, I have started four businesses, which were two solicitors' practices, a lettings agency and an alternative treatment firm. I had to make a decision as to the best place for each to trade given available cash, the particular requirements of that business and my personal life at that time.

One of my solicitor's practices started off in my back bedroom and moved successively into larger premises. The current one started in very grotty offices and moved to better rented ones. The lettings agency sublets space from the business now and the alternative treatment firm hired room space by the hour.

So, let us have a look at the various options available to you when you are first starting up or are in the early years of your business.

The options primarily are to work from home, rent accommodation in fully or partially-serviced office space, sublet office space from another business or enter into a full lease.

As ever each option has its pros and cons. Be mindful though that as your business grows or shrinks over the years your needs will change. The firm who let our offices before us started in our 2000 sq ft, expanded into 4000 sq ft and then shrank back to the 2000.

Working from home

Working from home can be a very attractive alternative. Clearly it eliminates the time and cost involved in commuting. The statistic is it costs on average £6,000 a year to commute into work. That sort of money takes some earning. You will avoid the sometimes difficult and time-consuming search for suitable premises, you will reduce your capital expenditure and you will not have to enter into a legally binding lease.

You will still have to equip your business with the essential items it needs, although the initial cost of converting a room in your home into your office will be much less than having to equip a suite of offices. Working from home can also look advantageous if you are trying to juggle home and family life. One client of mine loves it because she is able to spend time with her young family during the day while on the other hand another found it incredibly hard to put any boundaries in place between work and home. It is not for everyone, as it can be lonely and there is no one to bounce ideas or problems off.

I did it for a time and was amazed at the times of day and night the telephone rang or the fax machine whirred. I learned very quickly that I needed two different telephone numbers and telephones, one for the house and the other for the business. My family were under very strict instructions not to ever answer my business line.

In making this decision there are tax and VAT to consider. There are some tax advantages in devoting a room in your house to the business. You can claim the costs of running that room in your accounts, you may be able to claim part of your council tax against the profits of your business and you can claim a portion of VAT on the fuel required for heat and light. Just check that it's OK with your mortgage company and that your home insurance will cover you, especially if you will have employees or work related visitors to the house. You will need to think about health and safety. You must carry out a health and safety risk assessment taking into account the kind of work you do and the risks to other people. And think of the very practical issue of post. Many people use a PO Box in an attempt to protect their private address.

Fundamentally, working from home is probably OK while you stay a sole trader but if you are building a team and plan growth for your future you will need space that belongs to that team and has the feel and character of your business. Having said that I know of people who have run, very successfully, a small team of people in the business from their home.

Serviced offices

The benefit of serviced offices is that you can usually rent the space you need on a monthly licence and most allow you the flexibility to increase or decrease the square footage you rent from them. Therefore you have the flexibility to grow or shrink as your business dictates. The majority of serviced office accommodation is provided fully furnished with a reception and switch board answered by a receptionist using your firm's name. An external caller will not realise they are calling a central switchboard, it appears they are calling your firm direct. Usually your rent includes the cost of electricity, gas, rates and so on too. I have visited some serviced offices in Birmingham where the tea, coffee and sugar were supplied to the occupiers as part of the rent. They usually also have a variety of meeting rooms which can be pre-booked with IT facilities, which is very useful.

Subletting space

In my other business we did not need all of the space we rented so I sublet part of the top floor attic to an entirely different business that paid rent to me and so contributed to the rent I had to pay to my landlord. This is very common with, for example, therapists who use premises owned and run by another business. They book the time they need and then pay rent either as a fixed sum per day or as a percentage of their takings.

However, many of the accommodation options we have looked at in this section relate to office-based businesses. If you intend to manufacture, store, supply or retail, clearly these options are not open to you and you will probably have to take a formal lease of appropriate premises.

Leases

I know from my own experience that it can be difficult to find suitable premises that suit your business, that are in the right geographical area, can accommodate your requirements and are within your budget. Once you have, it is extremely important that you take legal advice on the terms of the lease agreement that you are being asked to enter into. Make no mistake, this lease is a contract that will bind you and your business financially for years. You must restrain your exuberance.

You have found perfect premises for your new business. All you want to do is start. The detail of the lease is just a nuisance. This is where it is extremely useful if you have a business partner. There is every chance that if one of you is overly excited about the premises that the other one may be reasonably scared about the commitment. This is very healthy.

I make no apologies that this is one of the most legal parts of this whole book. Commercial lease law is complex and can have serious consequences if it is wrong. By all means find a solicitor, either by recommendation or by a local or internet search, and always ask them for a detailed quotation for the lease. Provided the matter proceeds as you and the solicitor expect, the bill you receive at the end will be the same as that quotation. With this purchase, as with all others, know how much it is going to cost you.

There is a new revised code of practice which was launched on the 28th March 2007 to help promote fairness in commercial leases. Although the code is voluntary, it does contain useful advice that can help you understand the terms of your lease and negotiate more favourable terms. You will find the code at www.leasingbusinesspremises.co.uk. The code aims to promote fairness in commercial leases, and recognises a need to increase awareness of property issues, especially among small businesses, ensuring that occupiers of business premises have the information necessary to negotiate the best deal available to them.

When you are negotiating with the Landlord or Agent there are some things that you must give thought to straight away. One of these is the lease term. By that I mean how long is the lease and so how long are you committed to stay in those premises? In many instances it's best if you can agree a licence with the landlord. This isn't so legally binding but it does mean that you don't quite have the amount of security you may feel you need to start up your business or run it through the early years.

When I was considering the lease for our current premises I gave lots of thought to the fact that we were being offered a five-year term. I felt very cautious about committing my new business to paying rent for five years and I must admit to having a sleepless night or two about that. However, I had to balance that fear of the commitment against the possible cost of removal if I agreed a short-term deal with the landlord. Also, as a firm of solicitors we needed a degree of permanence as clients and potential clients had to know where we were. And inevitably as part of our business we create a lot of archiving and storage. Simply moving all of that if we had a short-term lease was really not practical. I did consider trying to agree a three-year term with my landlord on the basis that we could have moved out of these premises at the end of the three years if the business was not successful.

This is a conversation I often have with businesses taking a new tenancy. A useful compromise is often that they have a five-year term with what is called a break clause at three years. The effect of this is that both the landlord and the tenant know that the lease will exist for five years but, provided the tenant gives formal notice at the right time, then the lease can be terminated after three years. This is a sort of protective halfway house that is an ideal solution for businesses.

The only possible benefit there could be in taking a lease for longer than five years would be to allow permanence for the business. As a legal adviser I would have to be persuaded very seriously by my client that a 10-year term was advisable and even then I would persuade very hard to have regular break clauses even if the lease could only be broken at five years.

The reason I am so cautious is that the tenant remains responsible for all of the terms of the lease during the tenancy period. In practical terms this means that if you have, for example, a five-year term and your business runs out of money in the third year you still remain responsible for paying the rent for the remaining two years.

Other than the term, other key areas of the lease that you must think about carefully include the rent, when it is paid, whether you have to pay rent up front, service charges, whether you have to pay for dilapidations at the end of the term, and your responsibilities for maintenance and repair.

A client is entering into a lease in December and with the rent deposit, the first quarter's rent, the service charge, stamp duty, Land Registry and other fees, they have to find and pay £20,000 in one lump sum. They then have the cost to do their business move.

And remember that cash will be tight. Negotiate hard if you are being asked to pay a quarter's rent in advance and a rent deposit payment. The effect of this is if the lease begins on the 1st March you will have to pay three months' rent up front in one go, plus three months' rent as the rent deposit and often more money for the service charge and insurance.

Here is an actual example where one of my clients took a lease of shop premises. The annual rent was £25,000 plus VAT so he had to pay £29,375 per year or £7,343.75 per quarter. At the start of the lease he had to pay three months' rent plus three months' rent deposit. Before he opened his doors he had to pay the landlord £14,687.50 and then another £7,343.75 in another three months. In addition to this he had to pay a contribution to the landlord towards the buildings' insurance and then he had his own contents and other insurances to pay for.

Service charges are an additional cost to the rent and can be a huge problem if your new premises are part of a block or a row of shops. You must look to see if there are any service charges to pay, how much they are and what services they cover, such as cleaning and heating. Establish what facilities you may be sharing with other tenants. There is a code of good practice on service charges on the Royal Institute of Chartered Surveyors (RICS) website.

Buying business premises

Businesses looking for premises will usually choose to rent but given your particular circumstances you may wish to buy instead. I know a firm of solicitors who bought the office premises from their predecessor firm with a mortgage and then spent £30,000 on an extensive office refurbishment. Their offices look superb but they have a huge financial millstone and don't have any flexibility at all. If their location turns out not to be as good as they hoped they can't just give notice and move. You have to decide whether you want to tie up your capital.

Chapter 8 - Basic contract and a paper trail

Ask for help. Don't abuse the help and be ready to help others

Congratulations

You've done everything. You are now ready for your first customer. I remember with great nostalgia, all those years ago, the first client I had at Allsopp Solicitors. That client gave me a cheque for £150. I was really tempted to keep the cheque and frame it but I needed the money in my bank account, ever practical.

You are now at the stage that many fledgling (and I am sorry to say established) businesses don't really pay enough attention to. It always comes to light when I am asked to pursue a debt. In the particular instance I am thinking of my client was owed £22,000. I asked for details of who their customer was and copies of the initial account opening information. My client was very embarrassed, they could not confirm to me which of the limited companies registered at the address they had on their file was actually their customer. We did manage to sort out the issue and they have been paid but there was a delay of about a week and potentially my client could have lost this money altogether.

Therefore this chapter is all about housekeeping. I make no apologies that this is the boring stuff, the admin that is not sexy and that you would much rather leave to someone else or not do at all. But I am sorry to say that it is a necessary evil. It goes straight back to cash. Good record keeping gives you vital knowledge and control over your business. You know exactly who owes you what, for how long and how much you owe in turn. You should be aiming for the least number of debtor days on the money owed to you and the maximum number of days on the money you owe.

New customer/client

As a firm of solicitors, we are very regulated as to how we open files for new clients. Our overriding requirement is that we must know our clients so we always have to check their ID, including obtaining a copy of any company Certificate of Incorporation. We use a company called Call Credit for our ID checks. They also do financial checks. You have to estimate how many you are likely to do and then agree to pay that amount per month for two years. The checking system though is easy and straightforward. It cross checks the basic information you enter against the client's personal and financial records. Then you can print out a very readable report.

We must always send a client care letter to our clients, which sets out the detail and the limit of our instructions. That letter explains the work which we have agreed to do for the client, who will do the work, the position of that person in the firm, the hourly rate or the agreed and fixed price and details of our complaints procedure. Our rule is we do not do any work on a client matter until that letter and those ID checks have been concluded.

I appreciate that as a trading business your own initial requirements may differ from ours. However, you must never enter into a contract to supply goods or services to a customer unless you know who the customer is and what you have agreed to provide. At the very least you should have in a paper file in your office a letterhead from that customer. Ideally, and particularly if you are going to supply a substantial value of goods and services and not be paid for at least 30 days, you should carry out a credit check on that customer before you do any work. Obviously you should not do business with a customer who does not have a good enough credit record or whose trade references are not sufficient unless you are going to do so on a cash on delivery basis.

I suggest that as a way of closing a sales meeting, your sales person asks the customer to complete the credit reference application and brings it back to your office together with an original letterhead. Once the credit application is approved you can then contact the customer to confirm the details of their order requirements.

A bit of contract law

There are massive tomes of law detailing the intricacies of contract law and so by necessity this is going to be a whistle stop journey through the absolute basics. Fundamentally, a contract need not be in writing. This is something people get confused about. All that is needed to create a contract is for there to be an offer and an acceptance. So, in my initial meeting with a client we discuss their issue. I understand what needs to be done and I offer to do it. I offer a fee and a timescale. There may be negotiation as a result of which those original terms may change before the client accepts my offer. We now have a binding contract. I confirm that contract with my client care letter.

Sometimes, the client's needs change or the circumstances change and one or other party may wish to alter the terms of our contract. For example, I realise that it would be beneficial to the client to form a limited company and have a shareholders' agreement rather than for them to stay as a partnership and have a partnership agreement. I would tell the client of this proposed variation to the contract terms and explain why. If the client agrees, our initial contract is varied. If the client refuses then the initial contract stands. In simple terms there can only be a variation of the original contract if both parties agree to it. One party cannot force a change of terms.

This principle becomes difficult to see if the contract is for example web or software design where as a part of the design process sometimes substantial parts of the whole brief change. In this instance it is even more important to be clear at the outset what exactly it is you are doing for this client and agree how you intend to handle variation on that original design brief – if at all. One of my clients allows two written sets of changes as part of the initial contract price and after that there is a fee.

In my experience the biggest source of conflict arises because the parties are not clear and haven't agreed who is doing exactly what and when. A multi pound production conveyor system fell into serious problems because my client, the manufacturer, and the customer just hadn't understood what was really required. The whole bad situation was made worse by the person responsible on the customer side changing and the customer carrying out inadequate staff training.

Yes I know I am going to say this aren't I – but please get things written down. Remember when you get into a dispute with a customer and you have to go to court you will have to prove to the judge the exact terms of your contract. It's a gift if my clients have written records and notes even if they are just by email. In my book *Protecting Your Business* I look in detail at the court system and how to take and defend a case.

What pieces of paper do you need?

I know from my own experience that it is often very difficult to create and then maintain consistency in your documentation and also to ensure that you cover all the legal and regulatory aspects that need to be included in documents. You will have a world of pain if you don't give this some thought at the start. And the problem will be that you will concentrate with tunnel vision on your sales and production so this stuff will come a very poor third at best.

What you actually need will depend on your particular business as will what you call the documents. But in general the process looks like this:

- Sales meeting
- Credit check/client ID
- Terms and conditions
- Written proposal/price list/quotation
- Order from customer
- Order acknowledgement
- Delivery receipt/delivery note
- Invoice
- Payment

In some industries, for example printing, it is necessary to have written confirmation that the customer accepts and approves a draft before you go to production.

The name of the documents you raise, their content and the format will depend on your own business. Keep it as simple as possible. It's a fine line between producing a good system that works and having paper in place for the sake of it. Many businesses for example can have their quotation and invoice on the same piece of paper. If you do this please make sure that your terms and conditions are on the reverse.

Ideally your customer should have a unique customer reference so that they can be tracked through your accounts system. All the documents raised relating to that customer will then bear that unique reference number. When the customer pays you then allocate that payment direct to the customer.

Terms and conditions of trade

I fully understand that as a new business you don't think you need detailed terms and conditions and to a very large extent I would agree with you. However, you may be surprised to realise that by the time you have concluded your first transaction from sale to payment you will have put in place some standard terms and conditions. At the very minimum these terms will reflect what it is you are going to supply to your customer, what will be done, how much you will be paid and when.

Terms and conditions can of course be complex, and sometimes they need to be, but I am a practical solicitor and I understand that the best terms and conditions are the simple ones which actually reflect what your business does, what you need to happen and afford you some security.

The most important thing is to ensure that the terms and conditions actually form part of your contract with your customer. To ensure this, the terms must be delivered to the customer as early as possible in the contract relationship. By this I mean that you deliver a copy of the terms to the customer possibly as soon as when you confirm that you will do business with them, after your credit check is complete. Alternatively you could deliver a set of terms to the customer along with your proposal or price list. It is very common to see terms and conditions printed on the back of an invoice. This is totally ineffective as by the time the invoice is delivered the contract is completed.

Bookkeeping

Your day to day bookkeeping can be done in a number of ways. Although it is time consuming there is absolutely nothing wrong with keeping a set of manual books. This is the cheapest and, at first, the easiest way to keep your financial records but as I found it is very difficult to juggle this particular ball with all the others you have to manage. So as quickly as possible find a bookkeeper who will keep all the entries for you. In my business we have a sizeable turnover and have a software accounts system, but we still only have a bookkeeper one day a week. There are many experienced bookkeepers who work freelance and are paid by the hour. And as an added bonus many of them have worked in senior positions elsewhere and they are outside your business. They don't get involved in the politics and the emotions so they can give you invaluable, objective input into your business decisions and finances.

Many businesses move quickly onto a software package. Sage is the most well known but it is perfectly possible to move from books into Excel spreadsheets before you go to the cost of specialist software. As with ours, your industry may have particular requirements which are best met with specialist software. Always shop around, though, and try first. I know a firm with a very expensive finance package that they never got round to using. No one had the energy or the focus to get to grips with it in the early days and handle the administration of logging in all their numbers.

Finally, a good bookkeeping system will save you a lot of money in accountants' fees. It's not just an urban myth; accountants do have to sort through black bags of miscellaneous and assorted paper in order to draft accounts for some clients. The tidier and more accurate your own financial records are, the less time they have to spend and the cheaper it is.

The VAT man

You should retain your financial records in a useable condition for at least six years. If you get a visit from HMRC they will want to see your records and if they find a serious breach they can go back six years and then a further six years! A few years ago I had a visit from the VAT man as he was then. Our VAT records were good and accurate but he persevered until he found an underpayment. Is it cynical to believe that he had to find something to justify the cost of the visit!?

While we are talking about paper trails you must put in place good employment practices as soon as you have employees. I go into this in detail in my book *The People In Your Business*. Finally, please remember to keep your agreements, lease and business correspondence in a place where you will find them again easily. I needed a copy of an agreement from 2005 and found it almost straight away. You just never know what you will need and when.

As I said right at the beginning, business is an adventure.

Avoid the pitfalls and have fun.

Useful Contacts

Business Link
w: www.businesslink.gov.uk

Business Plan Pro
w: www.paloalto.com

Business Plan Wizard
w: www.peterjones.tv

Code for leasing business premises
w: www.leasingbusinesspremises.co.uk

Companies House
w: www.companieshouse.gov.uk
t: 0303 1234 500

Her Majesty's Revenue and Customs (HMRC)
t: 08459 154515

Noble Manhattan Coaching Ltd
w: www.noble-manhattan.com

Royal Institute of Chartered Surveyors (RICS)
w: www.rics.org

For more information about me visit: The Law Practice (UK) Ltd
w: www.lplawfirm.com
or
The 'What The Solicitor Says' website
w: www.whatthesolicitorsays.co.uk

Useful Reading

Blackwell, E, *The Sunday Times Business Plan Workbook*; Kogan Page, London, 2005.

Dell, M, *Direct From Dell*; Profile Books, London, 2000.

Ferriss, T, *The Four Hour Work Week*; Vermilion, London, 2008.

Gerber, M, *The E Myth Revisited*; Harper Collins, London, 1994.

Godin, S, *Purple Cow*; Penguin Books, London, 2005.

Heath, C, and Heath, D, *Made to Stick*; Arrow Books Ltd, London, 2008.

Hill, N, *Think and Grow Rich*; Vermillion, London, 2009.

Johnson, S, *Who moved my cheese?*; Vermilion, London, 1999.

Jones, P, *Tycoon*; Hodder and Stoughton, London, 2006.

Koch, R, *Living the 80/20 Way*; Nicholas Brealey Publishing, London, 2004.

Southon, M and West, C, *The Beermat Entrepreneur*; Prentice Hall, New Jersey, 2008.

What people say about Gwyneth

"This is the book that I so wish someone had given me when I first started out in business. Over the years I have built and sold many businesses and the guidance and help that Gwyneth has provided within this manual is worth an absolute fortune. The checklists and guidance given here should be made compulsory for all men and women starting in business today. I intend to recommend this book to all of my business clients that I currently mentor."
Gerard O'Donovan, Noble Manhattan Coaching

"Gwyneth and her team really deliver! I had a potential issue looming and I was really impressed by how Gwyneth quickly rang me back, asked me a few questions and then gave me a few options for what I could do. Talk about quick service. I can't praise her enough – thank you, thank you, thank you!"
Matthew Moody, Stanford Knight

"Gwyneth and her team are truly excellent. The services she offers are professional and with that personal touch."
Edwina Silver, Warwickshire Property Meet

"Many thanks for the chat. You won't believe this but in those few short minutes I made some major decisions – talking to a complete stranger really helped me see things clearly. Most odd – you're like Samaritans for property investors!!! Anyway, thank you!"
Lisa Orme, Keys Property Ltd

"I love Gwyneth's new book; it is easy to digest and quick to implement. I wish I had read it when I started up, I would have got off the ground (and making money) in half the time."
Richard Barratt, www.richerimage.co.uk

Coming soon...

What the solicitor says about… The People In Your Business
Available April 2011

The second book in the 'What the solicitor says' series will focus on the people in your business – from managing co-directors and employees to suppliers and clients. Below is a taste of the information you will gain from the second book:

The Employment Act 2008 is a new piece of employment legislation which places great emphasis upon the parties following the new ACAS Code of Practice and Guidance on Disciplinary and Grievance Procedures (www.acas.org.uk/dgcode2009). The whole ethos of the new code is to encourage the parties to resolve problems in the workplace at the earliest possible opportunity and with the least possible formality. The emphasis still lies upon the word 'fair'. Whether the employer is dealing with a disciplinary matter or a grievance it is important to deal with issues fairly. There are a number of elements to take into account:

- Both parties should raise and deal with issues promptly and should not allow any unreasonable delays
- Both parties should act consistently
- Employers should carry out any necessary investigations to allow the facts to be established
- Employers should inform employees of the basis of the problem and give them the opportunity to put their case before any decisions are made
- Employers should allow employees to be accompanied at any formal disciplinary or grievance meeting.

Coming soon...

What the solicitor says about… Protecting Your Business
Available September 2011

The third book in the 'What the solicitor says' series will focus on protecting your business and will provide readers with a practical guide through the legal maze of the county courts and industrial tribunals. Below is a taste of the information you will gain from the third book:

The Late Payment of Commercial Debts (Interest) Act 1998 – or more succinctly The Late Payment Legislation – protects you against late payments. If one of your customers is late in paying then write to that customer giving them a formal notice of your intention to claim under the late payment legislation. You should include:

- How much is owed – it may be helpful to provide the total amount of interest owed at the date of the invoice and, if the principal has not been paid, the rate at which the interest will continue to be accrued
- The amount owed and full details of the original outstanding invoice(s)
- To whom payment should be made, by what date and to what address
- By what method the payment should be made eg cheque, electronic transfer etc

To calculate the late payment interest you need to add 8% to the published Bank of England base rate for the six month period in which your debt became late. You will find the correct interest rates on www.payontime.co.uk. You charge interest on the gross amount of the debt, including any element of VAT, but you don't pay VAT on the interest.

# The Law Practice (UK) Ltd

Free Guide

It's Well Worth Your Read!

Thank you for reading this book. It will help your business!

And my help doesn't stop here. Business can be full of legal landmines. They can and are lying in wait for us to inadvertently tread on.

My promise is to always provide you with legal and business information which is relevant, practical and useful. This is why I have written a free guide for the readers of this book. You can download the free guide at:

www.whatthesolicitorsays.co.uk/mines

While you're there, you can also ask me any question you may have on this book in the comment section of the website:

www.whatthesolicitorsays.co.uk

This is not 'just another book'. My aim was always to publish a series of books where you can directly interact with me, the author. I will personally take your questions and help.

I look forward to hearing from you.

Gwyneth